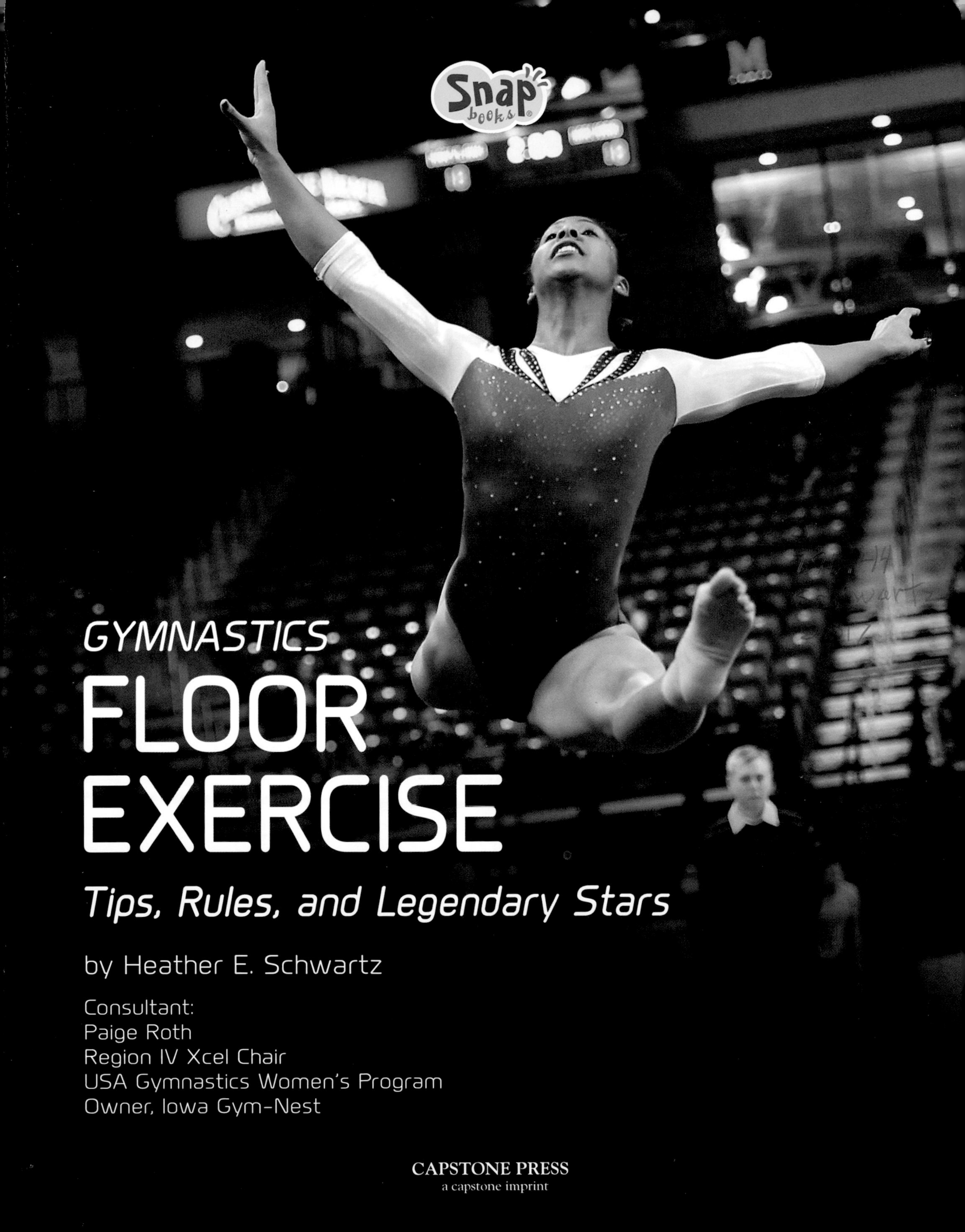

GYMNASTICS

FLOOR
EXERCISE

Tips, Rules, and Legendary Stars

by Heather E. Schwartz

Consultant:
Paige Roth
Region IV Xcel Chair
USA Gymnastics Women's Program
Owner, Iowa Gym-Nest

CAPSTONE PRESS
a capstone imprint

Snap Books are published by Capstone Press,
1710 Roe Crest Drive, North Mankato, Minnesota 56003
www.mycapstone.com

Library of Congress Cataloging-in-Publication Data
Names: Schwartz, Heather E., author.
Title: Floor exercise : tips, rules, and legendary stars / by Heather E. Schwartz.
Description: North Mankato, Minnesota : Capstone Press, 2017. | Series: Snap
    books. Gymnastics | Includes bibliographical references and index.
Identifiers: LCCN 2016001764| ISBN 9781515722182 (library binding) |
    ISBN 9781515722236 (ebook (pdf))
Subjects: LCSH: Floor exercise (Gymnastics)—Juvenile literature.
Classification: LCC GV545.3 .S39 2017 | DDC 613.7/1—dc23
LC record available at http://lccn.loc.gov/2016001764

Editorial Credits
Gena Chester, editor
Bobbie Nuytten, designer
Kelly Garvin, media researcher
Tori Abraham, production specialist

Image Credits
Capstone Press: Karon Dubke, 6, 8, 9, 10, 11, 12, 15 (bottom), 16, 17 (b), 19,
23, 24, Martin Bustamante, 12 (top), 13, 14, 15 (top); Dreamstime: Igor Dolgov,
21, Sasha Samardzija, cover; Getty Images: Bob Thomas, 26, Horstmuller/
ullstein bild, 29, ullstein bild, 28; iStockphoto/PeopleImages, 25; Newscom:
David Eulitt/MCT, 27, Mike Theiler/UPI, 5; Shutterstock: ID1974, 18,
Aspen Photo, 1, ITALO, 7, Lilyana Vynogradova, 17 (top), LuckyImages, 25,
ruigsantos, 22

Artistic Elements: Shutterstock: a;exdndz, Hakki Arslan, kayannl

Special Thank You
Thank you to the coaches and gymnasts at GK Gymnastics.

Printed in the United States of America in North Mankato, Minnesota.
009686F16

Table of Contents

Tumbling Through Time. 4

CHAPTER 1
Fun on the Floor 6

CHAPTER 2
Tricks of the Trade 8

CHAPTER 3
Routine Matters. .16

CHAPTER 4
Competition Time. 20

CHAPTER 5
Legends of Floor Exercise. 26

GLOSSARY 30

READ MORE 31

INTERNET SITES .31

INDEX 32

Tumbling
Through Time

At the 2012 London Olympics, gymnast Gabrielle Douglas made history in floor exercise. With her explosive tumbling passes, artistry, and nearly flawless landings, Gabrielle completed an impeccable performance. She walked away with a gold medal in the individual all-around finals. She was the first African-American gymnast to win gold in that category.

Gymnasts who tumble are part of a gymnastics discipline with a long history. Tumbling has roots that extend thousands of years. Ancient civilizations performed it as entertainment. These performances took place in China, Egypt, Greece, and Persia.

Tumbling became a sport much later, although it still wasn't considered part of gymnastics. Men competed in tumbling only once as a standalone event in the 1932 Olympic Games.

Today, tumbling is part of the floor exercise artistic gymnastics event. Since the 1952 Olympic Games, both men and women have competed in the event. Gymnasts work their skills on the floor and in the air. They perform challenging moves such as rolls, flips, handsprings, and walkovers.

Fast Fact:
Men and women gymnasts compete in only two mutual events—floor exercise and vault. The rest of the events in artistic gymnastics are gender-specific.

*Gabrielle Douglas at the
2012 Olympics*

CHAPTER 1

Fun on the
Floor

Floor exercise routines are thrilling to watch, fun to perform, and challenging to perfect. It all starts with learning tumbling skills.

Experienced gymnasts make tumbling look easy. But don't be fooled. It takes time and tons of practice to get the moves right. All practice should take place in a gym with a professional coach or **spotter** by your side. It's the only way to train safely and prevent injury.

Gymnasts can get started by finding a gymnastics club in their area. USA Gymnastics lists member gyms on their website. The Amateur Athletic Union (AAU) also runs programs and competitions in trampoline and tumbling as a combined sport.

At a club you can connect with a coach. From there you can start learning tumbling moves and maybe one day compete in floor exercise.

spotter—a person who keeps watch to help prevent injury

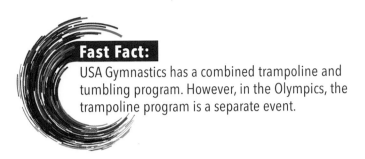

CHAPTER 2

Tricks
of the Trade

Gymnasts start learning basic tumbling skills for floor exercise. They develop the flexibility and strength needed to make shapes with their body. At first, it all takes place on the floor.

Basic tumbling skills include:

Arabesque

Stand on one leg, keeping that leg straight or slightly bent. Extend your arms to your sides. Raise the other leg behind your back, keeping it straight.

Forward Roll

Squat on the floor. Bend forward and put your hands on the ground. Tuck your head between your hands. Roll forward so your hips go over your head. Keep legs straight and toes pointed. Use your **momentum** to finish in a standing position. Do not use your hands to push yourself up.

momentum—the force or speed created by movement

Stretch First

Always prepare your muscles for gymnastic moves by stretching first. Stretching helps improve flexibility so you can perform better. Your coach can teach you specific stretches that will help with each skill. Your coach may even recommend stretches you can safely do at home.

Modified Moves

Many basic tumbling skills help gymnasts learn more difficult moves later on. Learning a bridge, for example, can help a gymnast learn a backbend.

Gymnasts also learn more difficult moves by **modifying** them. For example, they can learn to perform a handstand up against a wall to help with balance. Once they gain confidence and ability, they perform the skill without a wall support.

After joining a gymnastics club, you'll likely be practicing these basic moves:

modify—to change in some way

Bridge

Lie on the ground on your back. Bend your knees up and put your hands by your ears, palms down. Your fingers should be pointing toward your feet. Push your body up to create the bridge position.

Backbend

Stand with legs a little wider than shoulder width apart. Extend your arms over your head. Look up and push your hips forward. Bend backward until your hands reach the floor.

Gymnasts wear practice clothing that allows them to move easily. Female gymnasts wear leotards with long, short, or no sleeves. They sometimes wear spandex shorts over their leotards. Male gymnasts usually practice in shorts and a T-shirt or tank top. Gymnasts may wear special gymnastics shoes, socks, or practice in their bare feet. Other footwear is too slippery and considered unsafe.

Handstand

You can learn proper handstand form by first using a wall for support. Once you feel comfortable, practice a handstand without the wall. Stand in a lunge position with one leg forward and your arms extended up over your head. As you place your hands on the floor, kick your feet over your head. Arms should be straight. Keep your stomach tight. This will help you remain balanced.

Moves in Motion

Gymnasts need to master each basic move. They can try more difficult tumbling skills as they gain muscle strength, flexibility, and experience. Every skill, whether basic or more difficult, takes training to perfect.

Cartwheel

Start in a side lunge position with one leg forward and bent and the other back and straight. Extend your arms over your head. Lean forward to place your hands on the ground side by side. At the same time, kick your legs up and into a middle split position. Continue toward the direction you kicked your legs up. Place your feet on the mat one at a time to return to a standing position.

Which Split?

To perform a middle split, the left leg extends out to the left. The right leg extends out to the right. To perform a side split, extend one leg out in front of you and the other out behind you. Keep your legs straight and point your toes.

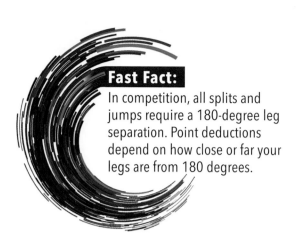
Back Walkover

Stand on the mat and extend one leg in front of you, with your toe touching the mat. Extend your arms up. Push your hips forward and bring your fingertips back. Bend into a backbend position. Kick your legs up and over your body into a side split. Let your front foot touch the mat first. End with both feet on the ground.

Into the Air

More advanced tumbling moves can bring you off the mat and into the air. Some start with a run to gain speed and momentum. Remember, these moves can be fun to practice, but they should only be attempted at the gym when you're working with a coach or spotter.

Back Handspring

Stand with arms extended up. Swing your arms to gain momentum as you sit back and push through your toes onto your hands behind you. Bring your feet up into a handstand position. Flip all the way over so you land in the same position you started in.

Front Handspring

Stand with arms extended up. Run a few steps, hop up, and lunge forward to place your hands on the ground in front of you. Kick your legs up into a handstand position. Flip all the way over so you land in the same position you started in.

Fast Fact:
The floor in a gymnastics gym is spring-loaded for floor exercise. It has springs built into it underneath the flat surface.

CHAPTER 3

Routine
Matters

Gymnasts who want to compete in floor exercise string their tumbling moves together into a routine. They perform for judges in a square area that is 40 feet (12 meters) long by 40 feet (12 m) wide. The boundaries are marked by tape or chalk. If one foot or hand lands outside the boundaries during a move, 0.10 is deducted from the average score.

A female gymnast's routine includes handstands, handsprings, cartwheels, round-offs, flips, leaps, jumps, and **saltos**. Dance moves must also be incorporated in the routine. The performance is set to music and lasts up to 90 seconds.

Male gymnasts focus on showing their strength and power. They plan a performance that includes most of the same elements, but it is not set to music and does not include dance moves. Their routine lasts up to 70 seconds.

If you want to compete, your coach can be a big help. He or she can help you **choreograph** a routine. It should showcase your strongest tumbling moves as well as your personal style.

salto—a flip or roll
choreograph—to create and arrange movements that make up a routine

Judging Gymnastics

The judges at the Olympics look at specific components in floor routines. These things are:

- choreography–how the moves are arranged to music
- artistry–variety of movements and creativity in the routine
- expressiveness–how movements and facial gestures bring emotion into the performance
- musicality–rhythm in the routine that matches the music
- technique–skill in executing moves

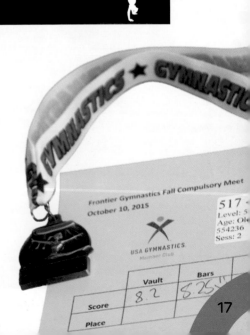

Moves and Music

Only female gymnasts get to take on the challenge—and fun—of setting their tumbling moves to music. The first step is selecting a song. You can narrow your options by considering songs that are meaningful to you. Aly Raisman performed with the song Hava Nagila at the 2012 Olympics. Hava Nagila is a traditional Israeli folk song, which identified with the Jewish-American gymnast. Raisman won a gold medal with the routine.

Songs for floor routines must be between 30 and 90 seconds long. They can't include any **lyrics**. Judges will deduct points for songs with words.

When planning choreography, match moves to the sounds and pacing in the music. Make sure to use the entire area allowed. Perform your best skills at the end of the routine and when you are nearest to the judges.

Fast Fact:
Female gymnasts originally performed floor routines to live piano music.

lyrics—the words of a song

CHAPTER 4

Competition
Time

Young gymnasts can compete in floor exercise in the Junior Olympics. There are 10 levels of competition. The lower levels are for beginners. The higher levels are for more advanced gymnasts. Levels 9 and 10 are for **elite** gymnasts who compete in national competitions.

The Junior Olympics uses a 10-point scoring system. Gymnasts are scored on the difficulty of their routine, the structure of the routine, and the **execution** of moves.

Gymnasts who reach the elite level in the sport may try to qualify for the Olympic Games. Gymnasts used to be able to earn a perfect 10 at the Olympics. The scoring system changed in 2005. Today, Olympic gymnasts are scored on two scales—difficulty and execution. Points for difficulty are earned depending on the difficulty of elements in a routine. Another set of points is deducted for each mistake made in the element's execution. The two scores are added together to become a gymnast's final score.

Fast Fact:
The official rule book for elite competitions is called the Code of Points. The Fédération Internationale de Gymnastique (FIG) updates it every four years.

elite—describes gymnasts who are among the best
execution—the act or process of doing something

Stick It

Judges require gymnasts to land from tumbling passes without moving their feet. It's called sticking a landing. This skill requires gymnasts to absorb landing forces when they hit the mat.

Practice helps gymnasts learn the proper form to stick their landings. The skill is about more than impressing judges. Landing correctly from tumbling passes helps prevent injury.

Strike Down Stress

Practice helps gymnasts prepare to compete. Even so, it's normal to feel some jitters beforehand. Gymnasts take care of their bodies to help beat performance **anxiety**.

It's important for gymnasts to get enough sleep. Sleep deprivation can cause stress even for people who aren't getting ready to compete. Teen gymnasts need between eight and a half and nine and a half hours of sleep per night.

Fast Fact:
Stress causes physical changes in the body including quicker breathing and tense muscles.

Eating right is important too. Gymnasts need a diet high in
carbohydrates, moderate in protein, and low in fats. Poor nutrition
can lead to poor performance, which can lead to feelings of stress.

Mental health is just as important as physical health. Many
gymnasts use **visualization** techniques to prepare during training
and before a meet. They imagine themselves performing their
routine and picture each move in detail. Throughout the exercise,
they see themselves performing perfectly. This type of visualization
builds confidence so that they can perform well during competition.

anxiety—a feeling of worry or fear
carbohydrate—a substance found in foods such as bread,
    rice, cereal, and potatoes that gives you energy
visualization—the act of imagining or forming a
    mental picture

Pack it Up

Imagine arriving at your competition and realizing you left some important items back home. You don't have a water bottle or a hair tie.

Now imagine getting there with everything you need in your gym bag. That's much more relaxing, right? Preparing ahead of time is a great way to reduce stress on the day you compete.

Make sure to bring water and a healthy snack. Pack wrist guards or tape if you need them. Bring bands and bobby pins to secure long hair away from your face and deodorant to apply before and after your events. You'll also need to bring a jacket and gym pants. They keep your muscles warm while you are waiting to perform.

Don't leave packing your bag until the last minute. Get ready the night before, and you'll avoid rushing around in a panic on the day of your competition.

Fast Fact:
Gymnasts are required to pull their hair back tightly for safety reasons. They need to make sure hair won't block their vision while doing their moves.

CHAPTER 5

Legends
of Floor Exercise

Many of the world's most impressive gymnasts are drawn to compete in the floor exercise event. Some of these gymnasts have become legends in the event.

Ecaterina Szabo

Ecaterina Szabo started doing gymnastics when she was about 5 years old. At age 6, she started training professionally.

In 1984 Ecaterina won several Olympic medals for Romania, including a gold in women's floor exercise. Ecaterina retired from gymnastics in 1988. She moved to France. In 2000 she was inducted into the International Gymnastics Hall of Fame. A kindergarten and a sports arena in Romania were named after her to honor her achievements.

Alexandra 'Aly' Raisman

Alexandra Raisman started gymnastics as a toddler. As she grew up, she took the sport seriously. In her senior year of high school, she spent seven hours a day at the gym. Her workouts included climbing ropes without using her legs while wearing 10-pound (4.5-kilograms) weights.

Aly earned a spot on the U.S. Olympic women's team when she was 18 years old. She was made team captain. At the 2012 Games, she won a gold medal in the women's floor exercise event. She became the first U.S. gymnast ever to do so.

Viktor Chukarin

Viktor Chukarin's path to greatness in gymnastics was not an easy one. His athletic career took a detour during World War II (1939-1945). He was a soldier for the Soviet Union and a prisoner of war for four years before he could return to gymnastics.

When Viktor returned to his sport, he trained to compete in the Olympic Games. He competed in the 1952 Games at age 30. He competed again at the 1956 Games. He won several medals at the Games, including a silver in floor exercise in 1956. His career span as an athlete, as well as his medal count, makes him a legendary gymnast.

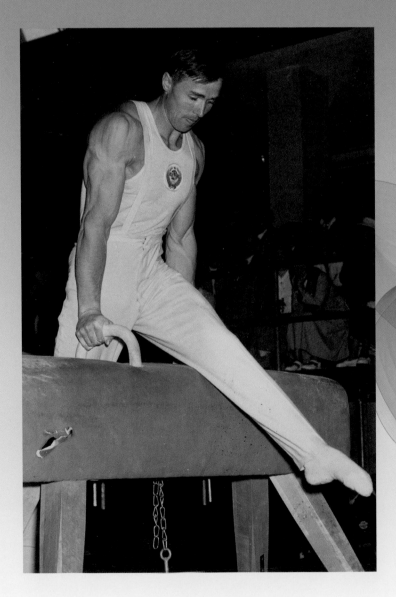

Sawao Kato

Sawao Kato did not show natural talent as an athlete when he was a child. But he was a hard-working student. When he developed an interest in gymnastics, he worked hard at that too. He started winning competitions and eventually began training with Japan's best gymnastics trainer, Akitomo Kaneko.

Sawao won medals at the 1968 Olympic Games, including a gold in men's floor exercise. He went on to win more medals at the 1972 and 1976 Games for a career total of 12. He is one of the most successful Japanese Olympians, and was inducted into the International Gymnastics Hall of Fame in 2001.

Whether practicing or competing, gymnasts who train in tumbling skills always benefit as athletes. They learn to improve their moves, face their fears, and most importantly, have fun with floor exercises.

GLOSSARY

anxiety (ang-ZYE-uh-tee)—a feeling of worry or fear

carbohydrate (kar-boh-HYE-drayt)—a substance found in foods such as bread, rice, cereal, and potatoes that gives you energy

choreograph (KOR-ee-oh-graf)—to create and arrange movements that make up a routine

elite (i-LEET)—describes gymnasts who are among the best

execution (ek-si-KYOO-shun)—the act or process of doing something

lyrics (LIHR-iks)—the words of a song

modify (MOD-ih-fye)—to change in some way

momentum (moh-MEN-tuhm)—the force or speed created by movement

salto (SAHL-toh)—a flip or roll

spotter (SPOT-uhr)—a person who keeps watch to help prevent injury

visualization (vizh-oo-uh-li-ZAY-shunn)—the act of imagining or forming a mental picture

READ MORE

Carmichael, L.E. *The Science Behind Gymnastics.* Science of the Summer Olympics. North Mankato, Minn.: Capstone Press, 2016.

Savage, Jeff. *Top 25 Gymnastics Skills, Tips, and Tricks.* Berkeley Heights, N.J.: Enslow Publishers, 2012.

Schlegel, Elfi, and Claire Ross Dunn. *The Gymnastics Book: The Young Performer's Guide to Gymnastics.* Buffalo, N.Y.: Firefly Books, 2012.

INTERNET SITES

FactHound offers a safe, fun way to find Internet sites related to this book. All of the sites on FactHound have been researched by our staff.

Here's all you do:

Visit *www.facthound.com*

Type in this code: 9781515722182

 Check out projects, games and lots more at
www.capstonekids.com

INDEX

advanced moves, 12–15
Amateur Athletic Union (AAU), 6
artistic gymnastics events, 4

basic skills, 8–9

cartwheels, 12, 16
Chukarin, Viktor, 28
Code of Points, 20

Douglas, Gabrielle, 4

eating, 23

floor
  measurements, 16
  routines, 6, 16, 17, 18, 19
    music, 18–19

International Gymnastics Hall
  of Fame, 26, 29

judges, 16, 17, 21
  deductions, 13, 16, 19, 20
Junior Olympics, 20

Kaneko, Akitomo, 29
Kato, Sawao, 29

legends, 26–29

modified moves, 10–11

Olympics, 4, 7, 17, 18, 20, 26, 27, 28,
  29

packing, 24
performance anxiety, 22
practice clothing, 11

Raisman, Alexandra, 18, 27

scoring, 20
sleep, 22
splits, 12, 13
spotters, 6, 14
stretching, 9
Szabo, Ecaterina, 26

tumbling
  history, 4

USA Gymnastics, 6, 7

visualization techniques, 23

World War II, 28